A PLACE OF MY OWN

A PLACE OF MY OWN

Poems
by Mary Howard

SMALL BATCH BOOKS
AMHERST, MASSACHUSETTS

Printed in the United States of America

Cover image and interior photos (with the exception of the tiger)
by Mary Howard

Design by Megan Katsanevakis

ISBN: 978-1-951568-46-7

SMALL
BATCH
BOOKS

493 South Pleasant Street
Amherst, Massachusetts 01002
413.230.3943
smallbatchbooks.com

For Mudge

Contents

I. *Vinalhaven, Maine*

II. New York City

III. West Stockbridge, Massachusetts

IV. Just for Fun

I.

Vinalhaven, Maine

On the Vinalhaven Ferry

Gray mist slowly replaced by blue sky.

Houses on the shore appearing one by one

in miniature, like an electric train set.

Filled with breakfast at Rise and Shine,

fishermen went out early today—

some by 5:00 a.m.—

in search of a fine catch of lobsters.

Dinghies bob at their moorings,

while seagulls perching on the cabin roofs

of dories left behind

keep watch for the fishermen's return

or maybe just until a fish jumps.

Harbor Evening

Near the red pickup truck,
amidst stacks of crates,
two men in clean white T-shirts
are hauling, stacking, organizing
for today's catch.

American flags ripple along the shore beyond.
The sun, hiding behind a gray blanket of mist,
shimmers on the lobster boats
tethered to orange moorings.
Nearby, a sleek black sloop rests with sails furled.

The ebb and flow of the tide tripping
over granite rocks below my room
dulls the traffic in my brain
and lulls me into a deep sleep.

Wind, You Restless Fool

Wind is a sort of vagabond,
homeless, wandering, picking things up at will,
dropping them just as fast.
It can make flags furl and unfurl,
move clouds in a synchronized dance.
It can also lie very still as if in hiding.
When it comes to visit,
it is a welcome relief from the heat of summer.
In winter, its rages can leave the soul cold.

Lunch With Emily

In the black pickup truck
above the rocky coast, we feast
on haddock sandwiches and lobster rolls to go.

On the pebble beach
we pick up sand dollars and
an occasional heart–shaped bit of sea glass.

Choices in our lives
drift through our fingers
like sifting sand.

Three Gold Stars

Three gold stars adorn a red door,
the entrance to the Star of Hope 1885 building.
Its purpose is to house artifacts of the
Independent Order of Odd Fellows.

Tired of their confinement and full of mischief,
The stars escape into the night,
camouflaged by their shining cousins in the sky above,
meandering about Vinalhaven in search of a place to land.

A white barn appears above the bay.
Swooping around it, much like seagulls playing tag,
the stars land randomly on one side,
and, in so doing, one or two shrink in size.

With day breaking, they leave the lovely barn,
returning to their place on the red door.
All that remains of their adventure
is the indelible outline of each five-pointed star.

Rolling

The sound of the water,
rolling, rolling, rolling by,
mesmerizes me with its rhythm
like a lover I never want to leave.
All of those water drops
falling over each other
in a white ecstatic froth,
tumbling in the tide of the moon's making.
My mind is as smooth as white linen
drying in a gentle breeze.

Vinalhaven Cemetery

Local granite, stacked in towers,
scrolled and carved in ornate patterns—
Kittredge, Smith, and Brown—
tombstones engraved to celebrate the dead.
Some were men of the sea,
others, soldiers of wars long since passed,
many with stories, passages from books they wrote.
Poems and quotations from the Bible,
"A time to weep and a time to laugh,
A time to mourn and a time to dance."
Surrounded by wives, children, grandchildren,
uncles, aunts, and cousins.
All buried within cut granite family borders,
gracefully set to rest on the hill
overlooking the protected inlet.
Flowers and flags wave in the ocean breeze,
a celebration of people I never knew.

The Spirit of Rocks

The spirit of rocks, dense with wisdom
collected over centuries,
absorbing time and thought
like great gods, listening—
the Unmoved Mover of sorts.
Unlike the wind and water,
which move with infantile restlessness,
rocks appear oblivious,
as if knowing they will remain
long after I have gone.
Perhaps they will remain forever.

Vinalhaven Haiku

Storm

The seagulls have gone
knowing the storm is coming
through the jet-black sky.

The Inlet

The inlet below
in slack tide at six o'clock
water bares the rocks.

Deep Blue

Isabel woke up early
as the sun was coming up across the field.
The path, well-trodden, formed a part in the long beach
grasses
leading to the dunes.
She could see the blue line beyond,
even in the early morning mist.
The blue of the ocean often startled her
with its intensity.

She made her bed and closed the windows.
The kitchen was neat enough.
Burrow had died last year, so there was no dog to feed.
Jake's ashes were safely stored in a jar on the mantelpiece.
Reaching for it, she was surprised by its weight.
Today is the day, she thought,
for Jake to go swimming with the porgies and bluefish,
in the sea he loved so much—
he had been a wonderful husband.

As she walked across the dunes, she felt a tug to swim.

How could she not join Jake one last time?

No need to worry about a bathing suit,

no one would be up at this hour,

and by now she was so old, no one would care.

The sand was cool on her feet and, at the water's edge,

wet and deep, filling the gaps between her toes.

The waves sparkled at the crest,

beaconing her to come enjoy its splendor.

In you go, Jake, and then she joined him.

As she swam out into the deep water,

she knew she wasn't going back to shore.

With each stroke she sank deeper,

not sure if before the last breath

she would see the sun

reaching through the waves

to catch her on her descent.

And then the deep blue

pulled her under.

When the Fog Rolls In

When the fog rolls in across the bay,
it is otherworldly.
Distant lights appear as Martian eyes
amidst the deep mist of sea.
Foghorns call to no one,
anchor chains are resting slack.
No sense of gravity.
Where is up?
Where is down?
Without stars to navigate and no GPS,
a boat could be lost in a sea of gray—
drifting aimlessly until it hits a rock,
maybe disturbing a sleeping seal—
or rolled up onto a shoal
or pulled by the current out to sea.
Many a boat lost that way,
so the captains tell
when the fog rolls in.

Sail Away Home

Like the sun and the wind and the end of a song,
like herons and blackbirds, the moon and the tide,
once or a second, many or two,
forever and now are one and the same,
wind-blown sails, a whisper, a name.

Dog-dashed whiskers blow in the breeze,
a lick on the nose, a dash to the field.
Farm furrows turn, the hum of a plow,
flowers and dewdrops on marigolds found,
a sweep in the air, the clouds chase the sun.

Sing out the soul's song, turn upside down.
Oceans roll frothy, sand in the shoe,
sail away, sail away, sail away home,
fly past the waves, a seagull, a shroud,
strings of the heartbeat, to home be bound.

A Place of My Own

Let me find a place
by the sea
where white clapboard
meets the rocks
and waves froth
from places far away.

Let there be peace
in my heart
and warmth in my hands
so I can write in the sand,
call the seagulls by name,
and leave the rest alone.

II.

New York City

White Clouds

White clouds above the city
stretch arms out wide,
holding the sky,
turning in sinuous ribbons,
mixing with wind.
Diaphanous gray edges
melt with delicate curls
above the hard-edged buildings of the street,
passing over the Hudson River,
soon to be absorbed into the night.

And Still the Bells Ring

Deep in the soul of silence
sheltering people keep
quiet, the empty street
wraps them in their sleep.
And still the bells ring.

Behind shuttered windows creeps
the chill of death's location,
within the confines of isolation,
surrounding them while they weep.
And still the bells ring.

Feeling empty, gone,
detached, beyond, away,
running out of things to say,
the television always on.
And still the bells ring.

On a balcony at six o'clock, a violin
plays to an empty square
to share with faceless windows there
the joy of a note, but not despair.
And still the bells ring.

Unaware of the bleak death toll,
outside somewhere, a tree grows,
a bird sings, a stream flows.
March flowers grow in rows.
And still the bells ring.

If death is to come or leave,
we, of flesh and prayer,
will celebrate the first responders
at 6:00 p.m., because they dare.
And so the bells ring.

One day the windows will lift us out,
beyond this shuttered place,
over the sill, into the clean air,
with laughter, to see a healthy face.
Especially then, the bells will ring.

The High Line

On the High Line above Gansevoort
plants form boundaries and pathways,
weaving through buildings,
tree branches form windows
revealing glimpses of the Hudson River
on the way to the skyscrapers of Hudson Yards.

Here flowers, once free to search
for clear sky, are now overcome with
scaffolds constructed to enable new buildings.
This was once a place I longed to walk
free, as if on a country road.
Now obstructions and dust fill the air.

Sheltering in place in one room,
I long for the High Line more than ever—
the music, the whimsy.
I recall the smell of the wildflowers,
the dappled cover of dogwoods,
the tinkling noise of their leaves,
secret enclaves to sit,
to ponder, to create.

Greek Names

Greek names derived from letters—
Alpha, Beta, Delta, Omicron—
move in waves of intensity.
Our lives lift with hope,
then are dashed with news
from some distant country
or state or province.
A curious thing, a virus,
wanting to live, find a host,
altering itself like a stealth bomber,
becoming undetectable before striking
those unaware or unprepared.
And so our struggle continues.
Masks on, masks off,
vaccinated, unvaccinated,
breathing freely, and some
not breathing at all.

Fear

Things bumping around in my head
and the walls of my small apartment,
I seem to have been here for years,
no longer counting days,
weeks, or even months.

Removed from neighbors, but not from fear,
sheltering, whispering to the air
as if the virus could hear.
Suspicion, anxiety, frustration—
alone, surviving the distances
and solitude.

Covid Haiku

Masks cover faces
still the dark of night prevails
hope lets us fly free.

In order to dream
first we need to breathe again
the world will open.

Yes, a simple word
pulls us into awareness
of the love inside.

Sleeping on Seventh Avenue

Seventh Avenue at night in the city
is filled with people nesting—
arranging cut-up cardboard boxes,
old used blankets, spare plastic garbage bags.

But this night was different.
A young woman with braids,
a childlike pink bow on each,
pink sweatpants with matching top,
arranging a perfect bed:
clean foam pad covered with a pink sheet,
duvet-covered quilt,
a matching pink pillowcase
with ruffles at one end.
An alarm clock with a cat face
sat on the ground next to her,
along with some lucky charms,
a backpack, and a pink pussy hat
possibly saved from the Women's March,
texting someone before lying down to sleep.

In the cold morning, she was up early.

Leaving her bed made, she crossed to the West Side

for a latte at Yanni's coffee shop,

then on to L&M Deli for a bagel with cream cheese.

Back in her nest,

she listened to music through her airbuds,

eating as I would at my kitchen table,

oblivious to the noise and dirt of the city

or any of us watching her from the windows above.

Pigeon Burial

I wondered how you got in,
between the storm window
and the window inside with the
arch and broken sash.

But there you were,
sitting like a homeless person
on a nest made from
little bits of found twigs.

You sat for a week, then so many more,
I worried you might starve.
Maybe you scavenged at night,
though I never saw you leave.

Soon you were all puffed up in the early spring cold.
Your eggs opened, revealing little pink pigeon babies,
lying with hungry open mouths
as you dashed about finding food.

When you left, your babies left too.
Feeling a pang of loneliness,
I looked deep into the empty nest
and there I saw one baby that didn't make it.

Wrapping it in a white paper napkin inside a shoebox,
with the sounds of traffic on 16th Street,
processional music for the burial,
I made my way to the recycling center.

Bullet Hole

Before I sleep and when I wake,
I look at the bullet hole
in the window next to my bed.

Across 16th Street, past fresh white curtains,
I admire the crystal chandelier
above your dining table.

I wonder where the bullet came from,
who was at the other end of the gun,
and why they aimed at my window.

I was the second tenant.
I didn't know the first—
she left after one year.

Maybe she had a jilted lover,
or worse still, maybe I had.
In the city, you never know.

West 11th Street

Will you run down West 11th Street with me,
past the trees, dodging snowbanks,
remembering five flights of a walk–up
and a sign on our door reading, "Nothing Worth Stealing"?

Will you stop to hear the clanging of oxygen tanks
being delivered to St. Vincent's and remember
the night you were wrapped in oxygen bubble wrap
under the watchful eye of the Madonna?

Will you go with me to the Famous Original Ray's Pizza
to order a slice with pepperoni
or maybe to L&M for a bagel with a schmear
or, better yet, a cupcake from Empire?

Can we sit on the stoop and share a glass of lemonade,
watching the dog walkers navigate the narrow sidewalk
while hoping to catch a bit of the sunset above the pier
through the tiny slit between buildings?

Wall of Moms

Portland, Oregon, July 28, 2020

One in the spirit, one in the cause,
the mothers gather arm in arm,
bicycle helmets, ski goggles, and masks,
a wall of resistance
against the armed National Guard.

"Black Lives Matter," chanting together.
A mother knows what life is—
she has given it to her children,
and will not let life be taken away from others
by the armed National Guard.

You know they are sisters by their word
and their might.
Their barrier, protecting protestors,
will not give way to fear
of the armed National Guard.

We salute you from New York as we watch.
You are the Moms fighting for a cause,
for freedom of speech and the right to live,
the right to object, the right to oppose,
the actions of the armed National Guard.

Naked Athena

Portland, Oregon, July 26, 2020

Naked Athena, stripped to bare flesh,
sits alone on the pavement in Portland,
possessed by her fury and defiance.

Facing federal officers,
who stopped in unison with their lights, guns, and helmets,
threatening her with rubber bullets and masculine might.

Her hair tucked into a black skullcap,
her face covered by a Covid mask;
in her heart, a non-black person of color,
her pose on the hard ground, a perfect spread eagle.

I am Athena, Goddess of War and Wisdom,
Daughter of Zeus.
I dare you to question my peaceful, naked protest.
Black lives matter, and your threats, officers, do not.

George Floyd, you breathe through me.

Burka

It is dark, hot,
I can barely breathe.
The space in front of my nose
is devoid of air.
Through a slit
I see things I know—
my neighbor's gate,
the street, the market.
Lowering my eyes—
this is outside, forbidden—
I disappear into nothingness,
a veiled thing that moves.
I don't want to be stoned
or beaten
or left to die.
My burka
is a suffocating shroud,
but to protect my family,
I will wear it like a flag.

Genius

There was a time, before molecules and atoms,
when the sun was thought to move around the Earth
and it was thought planets might be stars.
Those few who dared, theorized
were doubted—
others thought them quite insane.
But always, curiosity has led eager brains
to challenge the norm, the established rule,
to question what is true,
not worrying if they are wrong.
Inside, a little voice asks,
"What if?"
Energy, mass, space, time,
light waves and lightning,
nanoparticles, gravity, magnets—
all having a conversation at one time.
A wonder, really,
genius.

New York Haiku

Snow

The sound of snowplows
children throw snowballs, giggle
white turns black quickly.

St. Vincent's

Oxygen tanks clang
at St. Vincent's lifesaving
Holy Mary prays.

Police

Footsteps of horses
clip-clop on the cobblestones
comfort of police.

Albino Manca

Albino Manca
chipping marble eagle wings
for Battery Park.

Rooftop View

In the city,
flat, neglected roofs and
water towers,
tin, asphalt, dirt,
longing to be replaced,
waiting to be filled
with flowers and trees.
A place to dance,
celebrate the sunset,
sip a glass, absorb
the dimming evening light.
Look down from above,
peopled sidewalks moving.
Look across, the other side,
dining, sleeping—amusing
to the voyeur's eye.
Look up, the universe,
expanding,
awakened stars kiss the sky.

III.

West Stockbridge, Massachusetts

Rain

Rain brings yellow, a gift of gold
from the trees to the ground,
where yesterday parched dirt cried for relief
and thirsty flowers stooped to fall.

Now water cascades past the windows of my study
as I write, rain falling like ocean waves cresting.
Darting shadows wrap each page
with flickering, wet, translucent light.

Fall is everything falling; still,
the leaves, the rain, the sound of a
soothing *shhh* all around
makes my breath take pause.

Apple Tree

A little dark spot grew at the base of your trunk,
a lost twig and then lower branches,
dropping down as if depressed.
It wasn't long until your spring flowers were few
and your fall apples didn't come.

How many years had you lived?
Past the October snowstorm that claimed your brothers,
past the violent winds of climate change in July.
A sentinel over the wild garden,
you stood strong through life's changes.
Inside, you had a little voice:
"Live on, you are kind—
you love your flowers, your brothers,
your red apples."

Now I, too, have a dark spot,
wilted skin, and broken limbs.
But I also have a little voice within
saying quietly,
"Don't go, stay,
enjoy the sunset."

Spring Shadows

Deep blue–violet
on crystal–white snow,
shadows of spring
moving gently.
Fir branches of young hemlocks
begin to sway freely in soft waves,
an ever–changing rhythm
born of the wind.

After the Storm

Aspen trees turn silver leaves
as the wind settles down
to a whisper.
The last of the storm clouds
move their fat black bellies
over Smugglers' Notch,
giving way to blue sky
and white.
Rain puddles evaporate
from the pebbled path,
filling the air with sweet moisture
mixed with lavender.

The Sound of Quiet

The sound of quiet in the woods,
honest, pure.
Moon shadows growing slowly.

The pause of a squirrel, looking up.
Wind passes over bare branches—
neither speaks.

My brain resetting.
My breath breathing.
My heart gently beating.

Forgotten are the sounds of city traffic;
keeping pace with success;
the constant journey to find lost things.

This is a safe and distant place—
nothing to do, nothing to say.
The only sound is quiet.

Spring

Brave sprouts break through earth
gray mouse jumps over the sill
leaves are growing green.

New day starts with sun
warm midday eases slowly
day ends with big splash.

Will the tulip glow
or the crocus warm its head
in the light of sun?

Caught between two lives
caterpillar butterfly
longing to find wings.

Equinox brings spring
now Earth tilts to say hello
sun responds with warmth.

April Wind

There is something about the wind,
something about the pine trees,
the rain, and the gray sky.

The first daffodil flowers unfurl
gradually, checking to make sure it is safe,
that it is spring, and it is fine to know
the season has turned over.

But it is the pine trees that catch my attention—
soft, full, warm—
swaying side to side,
surrounding me like a magic blanket.

Two Fawns in the Woods

With joyful leaps,
two fawns dance across my path
in unison as fluid white waves.
Maybe it was my feet crunching the ice
beneath the snow
that stirred such wonder.
Or maybe it was just the joy
of a new spring day
when the woods awakened.
I would have followed but
had to turn down the hill
through the small opening in the trees
towards the river and the sparkle of sunlight.
I wonder where you will prance next;
I wonder the same for me.

Steps

I count your steps on the stairs,
one to ten,
making sure you don't miss any
and fall on the ficus tree at the bottom
or onto the little table
with the ceramic donkey lamp
left on so you can see
in the dark, shadowy
middle of the night.
I count the millions of ways
I love you with each step,
moving towards
I am not sure what
or where
or how
the end will be.

A Path

If there is a little space
between the branches of the trees,
I might be able to walk
that path to the sky beyond.

The freedom of the choice
to stay or climb the ladder—
an opportunity to reach
past that imagined ceiling awaits.

To dare to leave a familiar place,
to not accept what has been,
is to welcome what might be
without fear of falling down—again.

Your Room

At the top of the stairs
I hear the bottleneck
slide across the metal strings of your guitar,
your foot tapping on the wood floor.

From the hallway,
I see the flies tied so carefully
by your big hands—feathers, hooks—
fixed on the old wine cork.

In your room,
I touch the photo of your trophy bonefish,
sailboats we chartered,
my surprise birthday party.

I wish you were still here;
maybe you still are.
I hear your voice at the landing calling,
"Where are you?" I reply, "I am here."

I Am

I am

the blue space between the clouds,

the whisper of wind between the stars,

the silence between the dog's barks,

the pause before the first note.

The only difference is

you are living

and

I am.

(written from the perspective of Bob Charczuk in Heaven)

Swing Low, Sweet Chariot

I can write my poems,
let hopes and dreams
fall out on the table,
unfolding like a napkin at a hearty meal.
But nothing I write can prevent
that night when my page goes blank
and the verse in my heart disappears.
Please stay, hold my hand,
kiss me goodnight.
I won't be afraid of the dark.
We will sing, "Swing Low"
until the last note
before all goes blank.

Angel's Wing

When the clouds opened,
feathers from an angel's wing
reached through
one at a time,
drifting peacefully toward the earth,
landing with comfort
in the palm of my hand.

Sheltering in Place

This is a time of sheltering,
a time of silence,
a time of healing,
a time for rest,
a time for reflection,
for some, a time for death.
As I passed by the river today,
a quiet voice said,
"He is risen."

IV.

Just for Fun

Quentin Chomley Bloxam the Third (A Fable)

Let the story now be heard
of Quentin Chomley Bloxam the Third.
As curator of mammals, I profess,
Quentin was the very best.

One night as the moon passed overhead,
Tiger awoke and left his bed
to wander carefully by the fence,
hoping that no one would take offense.
A hole in the wire clearly showed
the way to escape a tiger would know.
Out he leaped, longing to see
the world outside, finally free.

Quentin was fast asleep just then
as Tiger left his stony den.
Ah, but the roar of liberty cast
such a noise Quentin awoke at last.

Sensing his favorite tiger was out,
he boarded his Mini and began to shout,
"Where has Tiger gone
in this early hour just before dawn?"

Tiger landed right in front of the car,
having jumped like a catapult quite far,
with eyes glistening in the night,
giving Quentin quite a fright.
"Say, good Tiger, where are you headed?"
"To find a tigress and be wedded."
"Why, I can fix that right away.
Come with me, for it soon will be day."
With that Tiger jumped into the car.
They hadn't really traveled far,
when Quentin said, "Be of good cheer,
I have found a tigress near."

Quentin was a man of his word.
He was, after all, Quentin Chomley Bloxam the Third.
And so, once Tiger was back in his den,
Quentin produced a charming tigress named Gwen.
Congratulations abounded, good news resounded.

Our story ends here in celebration
of two tigers roaring marriage incantations.
And if little tigers come forth,
maybe one will be named
Quentin Chomley Bloxam the Fourth.

About the Author

After graduating from McGill University and Parsons School of Design, poet Mary Howard lived in New York City for more than fifty years. There she ran an interior architectural firm with her husband, Bob Charczuk, designing more than four million square feet of commercial office space. Living in a one-bedroom apartment, Mary and Bob raised their son, Will. After her husband died in 2000, Mary began spending more time in the Berkshires, and poetry became her primary focus.

This, Mary's second collection of poems and photographs, was written during the height of the COVID-19 pandemic, reflecting the internal traumas and insights experienced during that time. Trips every summer to The Tidewater inn in Vinalhaven, Maine, memories of her time in New York, and daily walks in the woods in West Stockbridge, Massachusetts, are the subjects of these poems.